The sea is the essence of Argyll, its real highway, and the Kyles of Bute must have been visited and used by ancient and medieval sailors just as today their sheltered waters are so favoured by yachts and other ships. This book aims to depict aspects of the area's maritime development. [1]

The West, or Kerry, Kyle runs north from a line from Ardlamont Point to Ettrick Bay on the Isle of Bute towards the villages of Kames, Auchenlochan and Tighnabruaich. The narrower East Kyle is measured from a line connecting Ardmaleish Point on Bute to Strone Point in Cowal at the mouth of Loch Striven. It goes north past the village of Colintraive where the strait comes to a neck by the Burnt Isles then goes round Buttock Point.

The Kyles separate the Isle of Bute from the Cowal mainland. The shores are thinly populated, and it is an area that is blessed by spectacular scenery. It has witnessed the evolution and development of the many different craft that have sailed here.

THE KYLES AND THE SEA

ALAN MILLAR

Tighnabruaich Pier Association Ltd

ARGYLL ✣ PUBLISHING

Published by Tighnabruaich Pier Association Ltd
Tigharra, Kames, Tighnabruaich, Argyll PA21 2AG
www.tighnabruaichpierassociation.co.uk
www.argyllpublishing.com

The author has asserted his moral rights.

**British Library Cataloguing-in-Publication Data.
A catalogue record for this book is available from
the British Library.**

ISBN 1 902831 87 X

Origination: Cordfall Ltd, Glasgow
Printing: Bell & Bain Ltd, Glasgow

Contents

Dulaters

Glendaruel

Arduchiran

skalachan

Mey

Achintaran

Kilmodan

Kirk

Levnakeil

Glenmessan

Achnaclach

Inschaith

Wig

Achalamun

Arduhalaich
Stronchulin
Garletter

Inverchapel

Blairs

Knockde

Finart

Stronspary

HOLY LOCH

Succoth

Garachra

Orchard
Dirnachvs

Ardnalucher

Coruisk

Cour

Achoan

Stonelonaig

venakinan

achandrain

Achagarran

Tamnack

Ormadaf

Shandeare

Achinbreak

Ardnacaples

Seorlan

Slagoch

Craig

Kardoch

Arran

harrossan

Calves

Rubun

Craigundove

Ballimore

Changehouse

Glenlassan

Lonyle

Arlaray

Corachraid

Garachuran

Glastean

Taynacardoch

Ballochyle

Achlonorars
Finbrea
Ardianandan

Dunlusken

Achmore

Biils

Stardecks
Clauch Pt.

Ladimgs
Ferry
Milltown

Stronsaul

Dunoon

Castle

kilbrides

Mella

Stuck

Carras

Yeragan

Glenken

Leeknagal

Shona

Gartanleists

Garrow

Craigeorachs

Kirk

Blarbui

Inverhallan

Tynuil

Bachan

Clunter

Greg

Porharlan

Braunoran

Cowstown

Fernoch

Achalean
Ardhy

Collarach

Bracklys

Burnackunan

knockamii

Bunakailie

Rue

Towen

Bute
Nakeol

Ardintraws

Southall

Glach

Tamnacks

Cuil

Kilmichael

Juntore

Newtown

Bull
Lock

Bullochreg
Shalunt

Culnashambrig

Stone
Pt.

Killellan

Red Loch

Glenmoris

Stucks

Ardmaleish
Point

Gortanmusaig

Hattown

Castle

inaland

BUTE

Kilmichael
Chapel

Lenihuline

Ardmaliesh

Ardmhor

Ardina

Toward

Achvuline

Clayston

Achahouk

Achmore

Blair
Ferry

Corachay

Kanes

Glecknabae
Lenihall

Kilbride

Kames Var

Cranslagmor
Gorthine

Badinbeg

Kames Bay

Port Bannalyne

Arbeg

Light Ho.

Toward Point

Milltown

Achalvorry
Stylage

Kilbride

Leighton

Eller

St. Colmac

Acholter

Arbeg

Bogany Point

Rattery

Achadlakennon

Gartnakaily

Cranstagloan
Cranslagrouatie

Largivrechlan

Ellepot

Rothesay

Ascognill

Isle of Ascog

Ascoghouse

Killtaveage

Ardlamont

Dunahint
Achintirrie

Foley

Park

Kerrycoy

Ferry to Largs

N. Kirk

Lamont Pt.

Point

Chapel

Ballianlay
Ballycurie
Quogach

Castle

Stuarthall

Mount Stuart Ho.

Kerrylamont

Inch
Marnoch

St. Marnochs
Chapel

Chapel

Kilmoris
Barmore

Meiknoch

Kilchismore

New Farm

Butts

Bruchay

Killcatton

Ardscalpsie
point

Scalpsie
Ardnahoe

Kerrydubia

Manse

Luhas

Temple

Kirk

Kilchattan
Bay

Lime Kiln

Castle

Stravanan

Stravanan
Bay

S. Kirk

N. Garrochty

Kelspoke
Fort

Newtown Pt.

N. Newtown

Cock

Popag

Glen

Laggantwine

Loch R..

S. Garrochty

M.Blair

Glen Callan

Light
House

Portachoil

ess Pt.

EARLY HISTORY

T HE CREATORS of what became Scotland arrived probably from Ireland and certainly by sea. Their primitive open boats of from about 15 to 25 feet constructed from leather stretched over a wooden frame may have grounded on local beaches. Curraghs like these continued to be used in some parts until the eighteenth century. Ashore, there are a few prehistoric remains: standing stones and cup and ring marks for which theories abound that suggest some possible interconnection, perhaps a lunar or mathematical influence, which might impact on navigation. However, these all remain unproven. [2]

(Opposite page) John Thomson & William Johnson detail from Argyll Shire Southern Part (National Library of Scotland EMS.s.712(17))

A Roman Presence

The Cowal Archaeological Society argues that excavations at Ardlamont have revealed a Roman influence and have decided that there is firm evidence that there was a typical Roman road there, [3] its route marked by various pointers: by cobbled kerb-like side bands, by the ways in which it was allowed to settle to a firm core between its hard shoulders and especially by the directness of its layout. It is reckoned to have run from north to south, from the wooded hillside towards Corra farmhouse near the tip of the peninsula and from there down to the sea. It was concluded that what has been termed 'the road to the sea' had been constructed to enable men landed from a ship in Ardlamont Bay to reach a fixed signalling station which was almost certainly on the high ground, on the spine of the hill running south from around Kames towards Ardlamont. Significantly, at Hunterston in Ayrshire, about fourteen direct miles away, there is what is also thought to have been a similar Roman-based road.

A Roman Merchant Ship

A Roman warship

It is argued that the Firth of Clyde in Roman times, with various interconnected signalling points, became a closed waterway with Ardlamont at the outer edge of a defence system established to counter the threat from Ulster whose tribes were then beginning to threaten Argyll's western fringes. [4]

There is some supplementary evidence. When Ardlamont House, a mainly eighteenth century property but with some very much older parts, was reconstructed in the 1970s, among the finds unearthed in its vicinity were various old coins which included *denarii* of Caesar, Claudius, Nero, Trajan and Hadrian. This temptingly attractive theory of the road to the sea seems to rely on ships beaching or even perhaps lying offshore on the dangerously exposed end of Ardlamont. But because it is a part of the coast that is wide open to the south and west from where the prevailing wind blows, often fiercely, that headland tends to be carefully avoided by most modern shipping, which is very understandable in view of the dangerous projecting rocky spit.

There is the attraction of a reasonably sheltered anchorage nearby; to the south east, just round the point at Blindman's Bay, known also as Ardlamont Ferry. The medieval and more recent road system certainly leads from there to Corra above which there is indeed a splendid site for a signalling station that might well have been able to communicate if not with Ayrshire then at least with the much nearer Bealach an Caisteal above Rubaan Point, Tighnabruaich.

It is not known if any Roman remains have ever been discovered there. So, while there is some evidence for a Roman presence at Ardlamont, enabling control of these strategically significant waters, it seems unlikely that many ships approached the place suggested by archaeologists; but they could, of course, have come in quite easily nearby. The Romans were not noted seamen. Despite inept methods of ship handling they did, of course, put massive naval effort into the successful invasion of Britain and one of their finest recorded achievements was Agricola's circumnavigation of Scotland in AD 83.

Viking longboat

The Norse Influence

Towards the end of the first millennium the east of Ireland and the western coasts of Britain were overrun by Norse invaders who left their enduring mark in place names, by a still visible genetic legacy and also in a widely adopted form of boat building: double ended wooden craft made from overlapping planks. These were built with a keel, which made a good setting for a mast and sail, and they could also be rowed and used as fighting ships.

The influence of Norse design has continued to influence boat construction not only in Scandinavia but also more widely. The rowing boat known as a whaler is a direct descendant of Viking design and 'canoe stern' and 'cruiser stern' yachts similarly trace their shape over a thousand years. And, of course, the Norse aggressive spirit aided the conquest of the southerly isles. There were certainly Viking connections with the Isle of Bute, also in Glendaruel and in the area around Loch Riddon (*viz.* Ormidale). The Isle of Bute came under Norse control but never Cowal to the same extent. Most local place names are Gaelic.

Glendaruel, is widely recognised to have been the site of a major battle fought in 1098 in which, contrary to the norm, the Vikings were defeated so that, reputedly, the river ran red with blood. There are also various local stirring legends from early history but the Glen and around the shores of Loch Riddon seem always to have been thinly populated.

The vitrified fort or forts on the appropriately named Burnt Isles in the Colintraive Narrows must, of course, have been connected with sea borne activity but despite thorough archaeological analysis there seems to be no definite date for their construction.

In more modern times there is no doubt that the kyles were used more regularly by ships of all sorts. After all, when Robert the Bruce lived in his castle at Cardross he went down to the sea in a ship which he kept for his pleasure and it is reasonable to assume that he came this way. Also, the Lamont Papers refer to be-flagged birlinns which passed by Ardlamont.

The Earl of Argyle's Rebellion
(Eilean Dearg)

A series of seventeenth century incidents much involved the waters of the Kyles, those that led to the Earl of Argyle's unsuccessful Rising in 1685. Its culminating point was the naval bombardment of Eilean Dearg in Loch Riddon, the major armed action to have featured in this part of the country, the Battle for 'One Tree Island'. Archibald Campbell, 9th Earl of Argyle had been greatly involved in much of the unrest, which plagued the country during the reign of Charles II chiefly because of the unpopularity of James, Duke of York, and obvious heir to the throne who was already a Roman Catholic.

The 9th Earl of Argyle
Scottish National
Portrait Gallery,
Unknown Artist

In 1682 Argyle was arrested, subjected to an illegal trial and having been condemned to death escaped from Edinburgh Castle, dressed as a woman, from where he made his way to London and on to the Low Countries. In 1685, following the late king's brother's accession to the throne as James II, Argyle then mounted his military expedition to the West of Scotland. This was designed to coincide with Monmouth's invasion of southwest England in the hope that the two almost simultaneous operations could jointly challenge and dethrone the new Catholic monarch.

In the event, neither succeeded, and both leaders were duly executed. Whereas Monmouth's Rebellion and the subsequent Bloody Assizes are well remembered, what happened at the same time in Scotland remains for most a vague episode in Scotland's complex and bloody national history. Argyle's Rebellion is one of many risings in the unruly Highlands but it should stand out clearly both because of the Earl's use of sea power and also because of the effectiveness of the Royal Navy. And, like so many other military adventures in the West Highlands, clan rivalry and, in this case especially, indecisive leadership, marked it. Had Argyle succeeded history could have been quite different. However, his defeat emphasised both the growing power of central government and, temporarily, a decline of Campbell authority. It also impinged on international relations at the time. [5]

It was then quite common for Scots noblemen and military leaders to pursue notable careers in various European countries. Argyle, however, was only a short-term visitor to Holland. £10,000 borrowed from a wealthy widow was enough to fund the purchase of a newly built frigate, the 30 gun *Anna,* and two support vessels; the 12 gun *David* and the smaller 6 gun *Sophia.* He was also able to recruit a force of between 100 and 300 men. It seems that the Dutch were apprehensive of England becoming a Catholic state like neighbouring France and were, therefore, pleased to lend support to Argyle. Indeed, William of Orange made a financial contribution to the costs of the expedition.

Argyle's small fleet sailed on 1st or 2nd May, and going north, reached Kirkwall on Orkney on sixth May and in due course Tobermory on the Isle of Mull from where the Earl's force crossed to the mainland. [6] Once in Kintyre he marched towards Tarbert where he was joined by a further 2500 men. Dissension then appeared and Argyle began to have growing difficulty in imposing his will on his subordinates and, in particular, on Patrick Hume, his principal adviser. Whereas Hume advocated an early move to the Lowlands, Argyle preferred to attempt to seek more men from his own area. However, encouraged by Hume's pleas the expedition sailed to Greenock, and having failed to win support there, returned to Kintyre.

While Argyle felt that he could rely on significant help in the west of Scotland, the traditional centre of Campbell power, reality proved different. For one thing, the Duke of Atholl, in the pay of the government, had been re-appointed Lord Lieutenant of Argyllshire where he had the backing of other Campbell leaders. As a result, the various historic enemies of Clan Campbell – Macleans, Camerons and Appin Stewarts – were all now aligned with government forces and poised to invade the territory of their ancient enemy.

In Lorn, despite the efforts of Charles Campbell, the Earl's son, only 200 men could be persuaded to come to his support. It was a similar tale on Islay where, despite some sympathy for Argyle's cause, the expedition gained only 80 men. As a result, there was a serious lack of manpower so that there had to be resort to the compulsion of press gangs. Add to that a complete absence of any detailed operational plan and Argyle's hopes were really based more on dream than reality. Although the Earl was a figure of some influence he tended to be indecisive and quickly proved that he was not a charismatic military leader, instinctively able to gain some quick initial military gain.

Growing dissension in the small army led to abandonment of a projected attack on Inveraray since the Lowlanders instead pressed for operations in Ayrshire across the Firth. That, in turn, led almost inevitably to increased desertion by the Highlanders so that the rebel army remained indecisively in Kintyre from where, after a few days, it made the short crossing from Tarbert to the Isle of Bute, a move which due to inadequate transport consumed a further three days.

Once the now smaller army was on Bute, Argyle's cause fared no better. A detachment sent to Cumbrae met government forces and was defeated as did another at Greenock and by then the government naval force had reached the Clyde. Carrick Castle at the mouth of Loch Goil, an ancient Campbell stronghold, was bombarded and damaged. Argyle's response was to move north on the mainland, through Glendaruel towards the head of Loch Fyne from where he then withdrew. It was at this point that the rebellion really crumbled and made almost inevitable Argyle's final march which he eventually made over the hills through Cowal to Loch Long, Dumbarton and beyond.

Naval power was the key in this incident. Without the availability of ships in Holland and the support given to him by many in Amsterdam, Argyle could never have got as far as he did. The deployment of vessels and how they were navigated in unfamiliar waters were fundamental. For both sides, it was very much a joint service operation.

The Navy, despite its small size and quite limited resources, reacted speedily to the crisis. In mid April 1685 there were only 30 ships in commission of which 16 were abroad. And, of course, communications then were primitive.

A Fifth Rater
by Van de Velde
similar to Falcon and
Kingfisher
(National Maritme
Museum, Greenwich)

First to sail was the *Charlot* which left Deptford for the Clyde on 3rd May. She took 27 days and reached Dumbarton on 30th May. On 3rd June it was learned that Argyle's ships were off Greenock so Captain Hamilton tried to frustrate the rebel force by mooring his ship athwart the channel to enable his little guns to command the approach. In the event, the flood tide was too strong so that his anchors dragged; but Argyle had in fact already retreated.

The next ship sent north was the *Mermaid* which sailed by way of the Orkneys with similar orders given on the 12th May to the *Falcon* which made good speed through the Pentland Firth and then to the west of Lewis, anchoring off Ayr on 3rd June.

Even quicker was the *Kingfisher*, which left the Downs on 23rd May to join the *Falcon* at Ayr on 5th June, having sailed by way of St Helens and Brodick on Arran. Also involved was the *Drake*. Subsequently, the *Falcon* and *Kingfisher* cruised roughly together in the entrance to the Firth and, in particular, between Cumbrae and Bute from where they spotted Argyle's ships by then in the East Kyle.

Argyle initially intended to attack the naval vessels using his three ships supplemented by 30 fishing boats filled with Highlanders. But because of a mutiny among the sailors, and with the plan vetoed by his committee, he withdrew his ships to the Campbell stronghold of Eilean Dearg in Loch Riddon. He was confident that the English ships could not penetrate the Colintraive Narrows, which would give him time to unload arms and stores on to the island. Meanwhile, Captain Hamilton aimed to seal the rebels within Loch Riddon by sailing the *Charlot* round the Garroch Head at the south end of Bute, up its west shore and into the Kerry Kyle. When anchored off Inchmarnock two deserters from Argyle came on board with information. Also, while here the yacht *Arran* that had been sent from Ireland to find out what was going on joined her. At the same time the *Kingfisher* moved further up the East Kyle before anchoring again.

A pinnace sent ahead to scout reported that five vessels had been seen anchored under Eilean Dearg. And, of course, with the complete absence of modern charts or buoyage and having to contend with the fierce tidal flow, the bigger ships had to warp through the Burnt Isles' narrow channel.

The government forces got news that Argyle's army had retired to march up Glendaruel towards Inveraray, leaving the castle and ships under command of a man named Elphinstone. Eventually, the *Kingfisher* and her consorts managed to negotiate the Narrows and it was proposed to attack the same day at 2.00 pm. However, immediately before this was done a small boat came out from the island with a flag of truce to report that Elphinstone had fled after leaving a length of lit fuse leading to 500 to 600 barrels of gunpowder, more than sufficient to destroy completely the island castle. The crew from a tender sent quickly ashore cut the fuse before hauling down some flags which were still flying: one a defaced St Andrews Cross and another inscribed 'From Popery, Heresy and Seizure Good Lord Deliver Us'.

It was left only to take command of various prizes: the original ships of Argyle's flotilla supplemented by smaller boats, which he had taken over. All were sent down the East Kyle to congregate together in Rothesay Bay where it was learned that Argyle's army had melted away and that by then he himself had been taken prisoner. The island castle was bombarded and easily destroyed so that today the rocky remains and surrounding water form an archaeologist's dream.

Argyle's army simply disappeared. For both subordinates and men little hope remained and desertion, the enduring blight of many Highland forces, denied the earl realistic military options. Even so, the Privy Council, though aware that Argyle's amphibious campaign had lost impetus still saw his force as a threat and reckoned that he might advance towards such important strongholds as Dumbarton or Stirling. Certainly, the earl had to make a move since, for one thing, it had become increasingly hard even to feed those still with him. The depleted force now comprised about 500 Highlanders with a further 700 men, mostly Lowlanders and Kintyre volunteers.

Glendaruel was the last possible area from where Campbell recruits might come to enhance Argyle's force and he remained hopefully there a further three days before, at Hume's insistence, marching towards the Lowlands. He traversed the Cowal hills and successfully crossed the mouth of Long Long near Ardentinny. Despite further dispute between Argyle and Hume who had advocated splitting the Army into three parts the force moved as a unit through west Dunbartonshire, across the River Leven and on to meet its end near Glasgow. Exhaustion, argument and absence of any plan, reduced the little army to a mere rabble. By the time it reached Kilpatrick there were no more than 150 men when, finally, Argyle was prevailed upon to make a solo break; but to where it was not clear.

Having forded the Clyde near Inchinnan, almost at the perimeter of the modern Glasgow Airport, he fell captive to one John Riddell, termed a 'drunken weaver'. In the event, the rump of the force, Patrick Hume and about 100 men under command of Sir John Cochran, put up a spirited but in the end unsuccessful fight nearby at Muirdyke and thus ended Argyle's Rebellion, on the same day as Monmouth, far to the south, entered Taunton.

The Navy's connection with this Rebellion was significant both because of the number of ships speedily deployed and especially on account of its impact on the outcome. While it could be argued that Argyle's vacillation, willingness to compromise with Hume, taken with an inability to measure up to the leadership example of such as Montrose pointed to inevitable defeat it is clear that for government forces it was a genuine combined operation.

In the background, under Dumbarton's overall command was the Earl of Atholl's army, but without the naval stranglehold around Eilean Dearg the outcome might well have been very different. Not only was the navy deployed rapidly and effectively but also a degree of disinterested professionalism was demonstrated in that the various ships' officers showed that their allegiance was unquestionably to the Crown Service despite any personal reservations about the new king. Towards the end of the seventeenth century most people in England and Scotland equated patriotism and the national interest with a commitment to anti-Catholicism, which, paradoxically, was what Argyle stood for.

Despite the mission having been pitted against the Protestant Highland Chief the Navy very clearly acted in defence of the state. Admittedly, within a very few years James II would be chased from his throne but in 1685 even if he was not quite *'L'etat c'est moi'* he was at least unquestionably the legitimate monarch, to which the Navy owed allegiance. Or, perhaps more simply, most officers, if indeed they considered options at all, just stuck with their careers and took a pragmatic view of the change of ruler. But whatever their outlook and degree of modern professionalism it was quite clearly the deployment of sea power which most determined events.

Model of the type of yacht that carried prisoners south and on to their execution.

That apart, the rebellion was put down with single-minded determination. Naval commanders paid little attention to any possible trade disruption by ensuring that all vessels on the west coast were stopped and searched. While the *Drake* patrolled the Firth of Clyde and the North Channel the *Mermaid* probed as far north as Orkney. Indeed, the mopping up operation was an entirely English affair in that a Royal Yacht conveyed those captured south and on to their inevitable executions.

However, it could be argued that overall, in the aftermath to the war, the Clyde area benefited economically with the evidence of many anchorages, including those in southwest Argyll, becoming well frequented as a result of an upsurge in trade. For one thing the restocking of grazing land to make up for animals slaughtered by opposing armies increased mercantile activity and many who had fled from Argyll to Ulster were persuaded to return home. This particular episode from history stands out both as the major armed action in the Kyles of Bute and also as a particular turning point in history.

NAVIGATION AIDS

NOWADAYS, the British Isles have a system of lights and buoys, which follows international practice, and in English and Scottish waters there are only two controlling Authorities. Trinity House, responsible for all navigation lights in the south while throughout Scotland The Commissioners of Northern Lights do the same things.

Until 1956, and for roughly the preceding two centuries, it was initially the Cumray Light Trust and later the Clyde Light Trust, which discharged these duties within the Firth of Clyde. [7] In the 1930s and 40s a regular visitor to the Kyles was the neat little *Torch,* the Trust's maintenance vessel; today, it is Northern Lights' larger *Pharos.* National and local variations have largely disappeared with the adoption of an international system so that now there is a series of lit buoys, whose shape and colouring conform to international practice which simplifies navigation in the firth's peripheries. This is especially welcome around the Burnt Isles where the two very narrow channels with their rapid tidal flows are clearly marked, even if there is an impression that the way is barred to any but small vessels. In the heyday of the Clyde steamers the speed and confidence with which, for instance, the bigger turbines especially went so confidently through the Narrows regularly amazed many passengers.

Although there were some early and rather inaccurate maps such as those by Ptolemy, Blaeu and Pont it was not until the nineteenth century that the Ordnance Survey and the Admiralty surveyed the land and sea. It seems, unsurprisingly, that many of the names now in common use were simply those recorded then at the suggestion and advice of local people. There is at least one record of a surveyor's name, as, for instance, with the rock at the north end of the Burnt Isles. Did Lieutenant R Creyke RN in 1846 perhaps find that rock accidentally?

At the same time as the Royal Navy's Hydrographer produced the first reliable charts, each handsomely engraved with offshore views of headlands and landmarks, the publication of the Admiralty Pilot for the West of Scotland cautioned mariners in its beautifully measured prose against the hazards of fast tides and dangerous rocks. Without such pioneering works there would never have been today's essential guides. Now, most yachts and small ships ensure that they have on board at the very least the respected Sailing Directions produced by the Clyde Cruising Club.

Colintraive in the East Kyle
From a painting by Mary Y Hunter
(Reproduced with permission of
Bloomsbury Publishing Plc)

FERRIES

THE DEVELOPMENT of motor vehicles and the advent of end- and side-loading car ferries has altered the pattern of travel. Throughout the nineteenth and twentieth centuries and for as long as there were steamers, and later motor ships, most scheduled services on the Scottish west coast, in the relative absence of good roads, were by sea, many over some distance The recent dominance of road transport has, however, revived short point-to-point ferry crossings.

By the start of the twentieth century most of the former passenger-only ferry crossings had atrophied. In the West Kyle there had been several. South of Kames there was a crossing from the cottages at Blair's Ferry to Kilmichael at the north west end of Bute which operated until around 1946. Traditionally, this ferry had taken the coffins of those in Cowal who had died of highly infectious diseases to be buried at Kilmichael. Also, the tenant of the Bute farm was required to carry parties across the kyle to Blair's Ferry. Blair was the ferryman and the name features in that connection from the mid seventeenth century until about 1780.

From Tighnabruaich there was, obviously never any ferry to Bute since its north end is quite uninhabited. Despite that, the local householders' feu contracts had a clause prohibiting feuars from developing their own ferry, an apparent relic of the medieval need for ferries' establishment requiring Royal approval. Then, at Blindman's Bay the eponymous Ardlamont Ferry went only occasionally to Bute since its main purpose was to meet steamers enabling passengers from the end of the peninsula to catch the boat there more easily than by travelling to Kames or Tighnabruaich. And long before the days of steam that ferry was a key link in the route from Rothesay to Tarbert with a crossing across Loch Fyne.

In the East Kyle the oldest route was, of course, at the narrowest point, from Colintraive, (the name derived from Caol-na-Saimh, the narrows of the swimming) to Rhubodach on Bute, where formerly cattle were required to swim the kyle and which now has what is perhaps the shortest car ferry route anywhere.

Whereas today the Government-owned Caledonian MacBrayne operates the crossing, its lineage is ancient. It was by this route that the Lamonts secured an entrance to Bute where Lamonts for long owned land at Rhubodach. More recently, Bute Estates, whose property ownership latterly extended to Colintraive, controlled this ferry.

Throughout the West Highlands, where there are more mountains than roads, ferries, usually driven by oars, held the country together; therefore necessarily, transport has been mainly waterborne.

The Loch Dunvegan, until the building of the Skye Bridge one of the ferries at Kyle of Loch Alsh, now the biggest vessel to have been employed on the Colintraive to Rhubodach crossing

CLYDE STEAMERS

QUITE THE BIGGEST change to the Kyles of Bute came with the advent of the steamship and the subsequent development of a regular passenger service and with that the construction of piers and of villages such as those at Colintraive [8] and Tighnabruaich.

It was the steamship, largely pioneered in the upper Clyde, which gave the whole Firth an entrée to the modern world. Initially, it was the developing towns within easier travelling distance of Glasgow which became what we term 'commutable'. The pier at Colintraive did no more than serve the small hamlet there.

Tighnabruaich was little bigger. The irregular calls of the pioneering *Comet* and its immediate successors of the Castle Steamship Company gave way in the 1820s to the scheduled operations of David Hutcheson, later the better known David MacBrayne. The activities of the various competing railway companies and others led to the outlying communities in the Firth becoming part of what was, arguably, the best organised waterborne transport system in western Europe.

The heyday of the Kyles of Bute was probably in the decades spanning the turn of the nineteenth and twentieth centuries, the years when Glasgow fuelled the demand for fine coastal housing and in so doing promoted an enthusiasm for comfort. At the same time the very remoteness led paradoxically to some industrialisation with the formation, for instance, of hazardous gunpowder works at Kames and Millhouse, which, in turn brought these villages, and Tighnabruaich to depend more on each other for goods and services. It

PS Lucy Ashton

RMS Loch Fyne
For many years the
Tighnabruaich Mail Boat

Duchess of Montrose

Diesel electric
paddle vessel
Talisman

also meant the regular use of the West Kyle by large ships bringing, for instance, the raw materials for gunpowder from as far afield as South America.

Around 1910 the mark of social acceptance for a privileged few was to have a villa on the shore line in the Kyles with lying off it, snubbing at a private mooring, a custom-built yacht designed to match its owner's aspirations. Dominating the scene, usually in Rubaan Bay, was at least one sizeable steam yacht. For those with adequate means, the apogee of development in the Kyles of Bute was in the years before the outbreak of war in 1914. Then, even in winter, there was something like a balanced population in the few villages and in the summer months Glasgow spilled out to enjoy the amenity.

There were, of course, collisions and accidents involving Clyde steamers. Both the first and second *Ionas*, bought by Confederate forces for blockade running during the American Civil War on account of their speed, foundered en route to North America.

Poor maintenance combined with the pressure to compete in races against other steamers led, inevitably, in the 1860s to a series of boiler accidents Then in 1878 the little paddler *Princess Alice*, formerly the *Bute*, was run down and sunk with an appalling death roll in the Thames where she had been sold. So often such accidents happened to vessels sold off the river when the merciless waters beyond the firth exposed the flimsiness of construction of these relatively lightly made ships. That, for instance, was the fate of the *Arran Castle*, which was lost with all her crew in the Irish Sea when making passage to London. It appeared that her boiler had exploded. Again, it was faulty machinery exposed to a winter gale in 1877 that forced the *Lady Gertrude* against Toward Pier where despite suffering no casualties she met her end on the rocks.

In 1879 the *Elaine*, returning from Skipness to the Upper Firth ran ashore on Bute opposite Tighnabruaich, sustaining serious damage but again no loss of life. Two years later the continuing need for an effective system of pier signalling was well illustrated by a collision at Kilcreggan between two North British boats, the *Guy Mannering* and *Diana Vernon* whose sharp stem sliced through the other steamer. In 1885 the *Vesta* suffered similarly at Greenock. Obviously, no passenger service of the intensity and frequency seen on the Clyde could have been accident free if only because of relatively primitive ships, the reckless attitude of many of their skippers and the embryonic state of safety regulations. The mystery is the absence in the Firth of any large-scale disaster with associated loss of life. That was perhaps due mainly to the accident of continuing good luck.

Before the prominence of the ship-owning railway companies towards the end of the nineteenth century steamers were privately owned and development of services was rapid, fiercely competitive and quite unregulated. There were accidents in plenty but a minimal loss of life.

In September 1886 there were admittedly multiple deaths in Loch Fyne, but these occurred ashore at Crarae, when a number of passengers landed from the *Lord of the Isles* to witness a massive quarry blast died there from inhaling noxious fumes The tragic news was cabled from the Tighnabruaich Post Office after the steamer's return call there.

Regularly, steamers raced each other. In September 1881 the *Sheila* struck at Innellan pier and badly damaged by the redoubtable *Columba* was beached there, a total loss, but again with no casualties. That particular race to reach the pier first had been won by the *Sheila* and it was to put a stop to such dangerous practices that the unique signalling devices were installed on all piers in 1889 giving local pier masters authority to call forward a nominated vessel when several were approaching at the same time. It was almost at the end of her life in 1966 that the curiously engineered *Talisman* suffered an inconsequential but embarrassing accident when lying alongside Tighnabruaich Pier. To general surprise, though the diesel electric engine started she failed to move. A jellyfish had blocked the cooling water intake! Passengers had to be transferred to the *Caledonia* beside her.

PS *Chevalier* spent most of her life on the Crinan to Oban route but was often the winter relief boat on the Loch Fyne service

Before some piers were built, especially on Arran, the only way for passengers to board and land was by an often-hazardous trip to meet the steamer in an open boat, as for instance at Blindman's Bay. These little ferries were regularly filled beyond capacity, often in a turbulent sea, but, once more, lives seem never to have been lost. The same avoidance of fatal accidents continued on the Arran service from Ardrossan to Brodick. Fierce competition and bitterly contested races between new steamers in 1892 led to a collision at Ardrossan but once more no one died. This was the pattern in the 1890s in other parts of the Firth where racing between steamers, caused largely by sharp rivalry between competing fleets, became endemic. To a degree it was inevitable since many steamer captains were, of course, part owners with a share in the takings.

For much of the nineteenth century there was a sublime disregard for passenger safety. Eventually however, public opinion forced some change, a trend hastened by the clear success of well run steamers such as the *Lord of the Isles, Ivanhoe* and *Columba* which showed that profit and higher standards need not be mutually exclusive. By the end of the century there was increased attention paid to general safety and at the same time a huge improvement in the design, reliability and efficiency of most of the more modern ships.

The remarkable passenger steamer service put these small Highland villages for the first time within easy travelling time of the city to which one could sail and return from in the course of a day. In the late 1900s there was a multiplicity of steamer liveries: Caledonian boats with dark blue hulls, white upper works and paddle boxes with plain yellow funnels; Craigendoran steamers marked by their red funnels with black tops with a white band separating it from the red; while the Glasgow and South Western had distinctive lavender grey hulls, white upper works and paddle boxes and a pinky red funnel with black top. Then there were the 'All the way' steamers and, of course, MacBrayne's mailboats with black hulls, lots of gold and brilliant red, black-topped funnels.

PS *Columba*
Probably the most
elegant and best known
of all the MacBrayne
steamers.
Built for and employed
on the 'Royal Route'
from Glasgow to
Ardrishaig

Today the road trip from Tighnabruaich to Glasgow can take under two hours over the Rest and be Thankful or about the same time by ferry from Dunoon to Gourock. The 'golden years' for public transport were from the late nineteenth century until 1939 when, at least in the summer months, it was possible to travel daily between the Kyles and Glasgow by steamer and rail. The boat left from Kames about 7.00 am for all intermediate piers as far as Greenock and then, latterly, finished her run at Wemyss Bay. This ability to travel regularly ceased on the outbreak of war in September 1939 and was never resumed. [9]

David MacBrayne Limited, for long a synonym for West Highland steamers, was well known for its attachment to the profit motive and how it prided itself on the prefix 'Royal Mail Steamer' to identify most of its ships. When the *Chevalier* on 27th March 1927, on winter service from Gourock to Ardrishaig, almost at the end of a long and distinguished

The *Waverley* calling at
Tighnabruaich Pier

service, struck a rock off the south east corner of Barmore
Island in Loch Fyne, the purser's peremptory cry of 'Stand
Back Now – Mails First' simply emphasised a key part of the
company's policy. Again, no lives were lost. However, the
extent to which this tragedy contributed to MacBrayne's
refusal to bid for the Mail Contract in 1928 and the subsequent
move towards the company's state control is not known. Then,
in August 1953 the three-funnelled *St Columba* strayed off
course in dense fog after reaching Ardlamont Point. Instead
of turning north for Tighnabruaich she continued straight
ahead and beached undamaged on the sands of Ettrick Bay
where the unscathed passengers were duly shepherded
ashore on Bute but only after their tickets had been carefully
checked and surrendered.

TIGHNABRUAICH PIER

A T THE HEIGHT of the steamers' popularity there were around one hundred piers at which regular calls were made, most built specially for that purpose. While today there remain, of course, modern piers at the major ports such as Gourock, Dunoon and Rothesay, all catering with adjustable link spans for modern car ferries, Tighnabruaich is almost the sole remaining example on the Firth of an original working wooden steamer pier which continues, albeit only in the short summer season, to welcome the *Waverley*, the sole representative of all the former fleets.

The pier was built in the 1820s to provide a stopping point for the Castle Company steamers. While nowadays the property of Argyll and Bute Council it was privately owned until 1960. Since 1999 there has been a Partnership Agreement between Argyll and Bute Council and the local Pier Association, which is committed to its conservation and continuance and is able to act as a pressure group on the Council.

It would be a loss were the Pier ever to rot away for want of basic maintenance since it is regrettably all to easy for perennially cash-strapped Councils to argue that prohibitive costs prevent such essential work from being done. For a while it looked as if that was likely to happen with this pier. Admittedly, there is minimal revenue from it but it would be sad for the Kyles were it to fall into the dilapidated state which, for instance, marked Auchenlochan Pier and the wooden end of Kames Pier that lay as wrecks, eyesores and hazards to navigation until removed by the Army in the 1990s. Were that to happen, it would deprive the Kyles of something that is handsome, unique and dominant, a Listed structure that, apart from its obvious function and the stated affection people have for it, illustrates the village's origins.

In the 1980s an independent study [10] assessed the pier's potential and concluded that because of its position in such a key sailing area it should not be overlooked. Due to its reasonably sound condition and also because of the spaciousness of the entrance hall with its associated side rooms it was suggested that it could easily and at modest cost be developed to provide changing, drying and washing facilities for yachtsmen who would also benefit from a pontoon properly secured to the north edge of the pier which would thus avoid interfering with any steamer operation.

Termed a 'Yacht Station' it was suggested that Tighnabruaich which by then already had a Sailing School, a Sailing Club and also a yard in which yachts could over-winter was an ideal venue for this compared to other sites in the Kyles, Colintraive or Loch Riddon which both lacked shops, fuel and more than one hotel. There seems to have been little local or government heed paid to this publicly funded Report, which, sadly, was never implemented.

There is no doubt that today's yachtsmen do welcome the chance to tie up to a pontoon and thus avoid the hazards of using a dinghy to carry goods and passengers between a moored boat and the shore. Admittedly, the pier lying midway between the Village shops and the boatyard at Rubaan is not perhaps in the ideal place since quite a walk is necessary; however, the *Waverley's* passengers are not deterred from marching along to the tearooms and village shops on Saturday afternoons! Of course a venture like this would have to be financed and run as a business, but that is another matter. The 1980s Study argued that the already considerable boating activity at Tighnabruaich could be better structured to the economic advantage of the inhabitants. If that smacks rather of a politically correct vision at variance with the reality of West Highland life there is no denying the growing popularity of boating and the need to cater for it in a way that does not conflict with the character of the area.

Boats already anchor or moor off the recently built lightweight pontoon by the Royal Hotel while off the Kames Hotel there are two lines of moorings Also, the former Transport

Tighnabruaich Pier on the occasion of the first *Waverley* fundraising cruise 2001

Yard at Kames old Powder Pier has been developed for the benefit of yachtsmen. Recently, the Pier Association has focussed attention on this unique part of our heritage and may have prepared the way for some subsequent maritime development. Had the Water Authority had the commitment, interest, finance and vision to provide more than a panacea when it failed in 2003 to put in place a proper sewerage system it would then have been possible to install on the pier showers and toilets, both of which are essential to any development.

And, it seems that there was once another pier in the village, in the bay at Port Driseach on the road to Rubaan, as shown on some early maps. It almost certainly post dated the main pier and because of its proximity to a house named Alma may have been built for the maintenance crews of Crimean War warships reputed to have been laid up there prior to being broken up. Certainly, the Kyles was a popular area for the Admiralty to anchor obsolete ships. After all, the unwanted HMS *Collingwood* narrowly missed being run down by Para Handy's *Vital Spark!* Also, puffers favoured the beach to the east of Tighnabruaich Pier for unloading coal.

Unwanted ships, moored in the Kyles pending either an upturn in trade or a final trip to the breaker's yard were for some years an unwelcome feature of many of the Firth's sea lochs before and after the Second World War.

LOCAL BOATS
AND CLYDE YACHTING

PS Duchess of Fife

SAILING has grown in popularity with the advent of smaller factory-built boats that have helped to make it increasingly affordable. More disposable income for more people together with recent technological advances have transformed yachting from being an exclusive pastime for a small minority to become a popular sport for many. The two decades before the First World War were the days before some felt that 'golf, motor cars and taxation ruined yachting'.[11]

At this time, with no television or instant communications, yacht racing, unlike today, was much more of a spectator sport, especially in the upper firth, near for instance, the Cloch Light and at Hunter's Quay where sizeable crowds regularly formed to watch the spectacle of races by the fleet of very big boats.

And, of course, the cachet of belonging to a 'smart' yacht club was deemed significant. The Royal Northern Yacht Club, then at Rothesay, regarded itself as being the premier club while what became the Royal Clyde Yacht Club at Hunter's Quay began life in 1856 as the Clyde Model Yacht Club, catering especially for owners of bantam racers and day boats, most the size of today's average yachts. Social acceptance was a key to such club membership and it was partially to counter this that the Clyde Cruising Club was formed by a small group of sailors in Rothesay in 1909 after some discussion which apparently took place on the starboard paddle box of the steamer Duchess of Fife while crossing from Bute to Wemyss Bay!

Today, of course, the Clyde Cruising Club is in many

ways the premier yacht club on the West of Scotland, responsible amongst other things for its very respected Sailing Directions and also for organising the ever-growing Scottish Series Regatta held each year in Loch Fyne. Its annual Tobermory Race passes through the Kyles each July with its periodic musters regularly filling every mooring in Kames Bay.

In Tighnabruaich The Kyles of Bute Sailing Club, formed in 1953, is in many ways a re-creation of the former local Yacht Club which had flourished at the turn of the last century when the Tighnabruaich Town Regatta was a more significant event than it is now. [12] Its success reflects boating's popularity and also meets a demand for organised competitive sailing.

Racing has, of course, been for long very much part of sailing on the Firth. In 1885 at a time when so many beautiful boats were being built it was recorded that the *Wendur* won over a course of 33 nautical miles from Hunter's Quay to Blakfarland Bay in a time of 2 hours 17 minutes, a record that apparently stood for seventeen years. [13] This suggests that that particular race was for some time a regular event.

In fact the Tighnabruaich Cup was one of the awards regularly competed for within the Royal Clyde Yacht Club.

Today, there are more moorings than ever before, stretching the length of the bay from Kames to Rubaan although most are for relatively modest and almost all for fibreglass yachts. The laying of moorings was always in these waters a private matter but in 1983 the Crown Commissioners began to exercise what they claimed was their right to levy a charge on those fixing a mooring to their seabed! The onus of collecting fees now rests with the Sailing Club, encouraged to undertake this chore by the offer of discounted charges!

RNYC Regatta c 1906
from a painting by
Mary Y Hunter
(Bloomsbury
Publishingplc)

Interest in sailing is seen in the priority given by the Sailing Club to introducing local youngsters to the pleasures of the sport. Tighnabruaich is, of course, noted also for its Sailing School whose courses attract to sailing each summer many beginners of all ages

Many local men in Tighnabruaich were sailors, not just those with the resources to own their own yachts but also the ones who fished for their living, in the days before the waters died from over exploitation. There were also those who went to sea in merchant ships and the quite surprising number who crewed, for instance, in the mainly Clyde-built J Class yachts and later 8 Metres which raced each summer both around the British coasts and also competed with the USA for the America's Cup. Many skippers and paid hands of the Clyde yachting fleet in its most brilliant years came from the coastal tracts of Argyll.

While the twentieth century's second German War inexorably changed life it in no way halted the affection sailors had for these waters. This was never more evident than immediately after the Tall Ships' 1998 visit to the Firth when a constant stream of sailing and motor yachts of all nationalities processed through the Kyles en route to Ardrishaig and the Crinan Canal.

Although building of yachts and dinghies ceased in Tighnabruaich by 1950 the yard at Rubaan in a revived and enlarged form now provides winter quarters ashore for more boats than ever before. Those seen and built around here have always been typical of those elsewhere. The ubiquitous dug out canoe probably featured in early history, as did the skin boat with a wooden frame, while the crossing of the open sea, as from Ireland, demanded a bigger version of the curragh. And, if archaeologists are correct, some Roman vessels must have visited the Kyles. Certainly, the Romans had ships bigger than anything seen previously by the Caledonians and their galleys co-operated successfully with land forces. Ptolemy's map of Scotland in AD 140, though cartographically inaccurate, includes some recognisable place names. By the sixth century AD open boats such as those used by Columba

A Gabbart
Typical of the small
trading sailing craft
found along the West
coast in the nineteenth
and earlier twentieth
centuries

were up to 25 feet in length and were mainly rowed but they could sail, at least before the wind. It was the Vikings who introduced with their double-ended long ships the clinker pattern of boat building, so universal until wood quite recently gave way to fibreglass as the most common building material. The West Highland galley with its smaller cousin the birlinn was essentially derived from the Norse pattern.

It was Glasgow's rapid growth in the nineteenth century that fuelled the West coast's appetite for leisure sailing and before then it was hard to locate any local yards where yachts were built. In Fairlie on the Ayrshire coast William Fife built his very beautiful boats, as did McGruer on the Gareloch with also the well-known yards on the Holy Loch. Admittedly, in the First World War ships' lifeboats were for a while built at Rubaan and Smiths' other yard at the end of the village street in Tighnabruaich constructed many very fine yachts' tenders and rowing boats which were so popular until 1939. However, there seems never to have been any clearly discernible local boat type. Round the corner, as it were, the characteristic Loch Fyne fishing skiff is associated with Dickie's yard in Tarbert. Boats seen in the Kyles have over the years reflected patterns common elsewhere.

Nineteenth century industrialisation led to the greater use of the Kyles. Trade and the carriage of goods demanded a particular type of vessel. Well-known and quite beloved, largely due to Neil Munro's Para Handy, the Puffer is perhaps the best-known West coast trader and it was preceded by the sailing gabbart. Perhaps not so much a specific type of craft this was really a generic term for small cargo sailing ships. They were generally gaff cutters, all with a high pointed square stern, low freeboard and moderate amount of sheer. Until the 1950s the ribs of some of these lay slowly rotting on various west coast beaches; their demise due to the rapid growth of steam on the Clyde

Years ago safety at sea had a lower priority than today. Lifejackets were rarely worn and, of course, yachts had neither radios nor modern electronic navigation aids. The RNLI was not represented in the Kyles until 1967. Within the Firth there were, of course, large Lifeboats in such places as Campbeltown and on the Ayrshire coast but there was nothing like the modern inshore lifeboats, largely pioneered in Cardigan Bay in Wales.

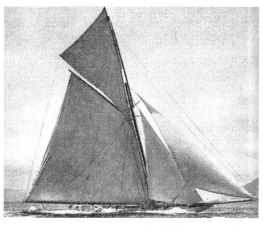

The *Valkyrie*, typical of the larger yachts that raced on the Clyde at the start of the twentieth century

It was a tragedy off Kames and a subsequent campaign for better life saving facilities that led to the establishment of the first local RNLI lifeboat. Initially, this was little more than a rubber dinghy with outboard engine. It was, after all, early days for reliable inflatables and this first boat was followed, in 1983, by something rather larger but very similar, the one which in 1997 was sold to the Sailing Club to provide safety coverage. This was kept in its own hut at the foot of the east drive to the Tighnabruaich Hotel.

To an extent, of course, it was the advent of the Sailing School and the growing popularity of small boat sailing that underpinned the case for a local RNLI presence. Since it was built in 1997, there has been a handsome Lifeboat Station in the Village street which houses the modern, Inshore Rescue Boat, an 'Atlantic 75', a fast Rigid Inflatable Boat (RIB) powered by two 50 hp outboard engines with a range of 180 nautical miles and a maximum speed of 32 knots. It is one of seven in the Firth of Clyde and has a fully trained completely local crew that includes both men and women. It is generously supported throughout the area by most effective fundraising organised since 1969 by the Tighnabruaich and District Lifeboat Fund Raising Branch. In addition to arranging door to door collections, it is also committed to what has proved to be a popular and well attended annual festive day held on the pier.

Detail from a painting by
N Whitla – a puffer
unloading at low tide
(Permission: Fiona Roy)

PUFFERS

THE PUFFER went almost everywhere: coal mostly, but household removals and all manner of goods were carried between Glasgow, Greenock and other ports to small communities up and down the coast. Their dimensions, no more than a length of 88 feet, were dictated by the size of locks in the Forth and Clyde and especially the Crinan canals These were supremely adaptable ships. With a steam crane they could unload on an open beach and operated away from home for perhaps more than a week at a time.

The Tiree, later Spartan, ashore on Bute in the Colintraive Narrows

Over the years about 400 puffers were built for more than 50 different owners. It was not until 1993 that the last commercial one withdrew from service. And still today the World War II built *Vic 32* is a regular summer visitor to Tighnabruaich Pier with its crew of working holidaymakers. Did public affection for this rather ungainly type of craft derive from Scottish early dominance of steam or was it all really due to Neil Munro and the *Vital Spark*? And of course, long before the motor car became ubiquitous, in addition to what came by puffer everything else was carried by the various cargo boats.

The vestiges of this life remained through the interregnum of the twenty years before 1939 and indeed continued for a few years after 1945.

The *Waverley* from a
painting by N Whitla
(Permission: Fiona Roy)

THE WAVERLEY

THE BEST-KNOWN vessel seen in the area is, of course, the *Waverley*. Built in 1946, immediately after the Second World War for the LNER Company and based originally at Craigendoran, the *Waverley* was the first post-war passenger boat built on the river. She is now the last traditional Clyde steamer. Her story has been often told: how she plied initially on the Company's former routes and also more widely on the Firth. Then in the face of changed holiday patterns the few remaining steamers were all brought under control of the newly formed Caledonian Macbrayne. Cal Mac inherited all railway and other companies' steamers and in due course, when there seemed to be no economic future for a paddle steamer, sold her for the nominal sum of £1. Optimists committed to her continuance bought the vessel and now after numerous traumas she remains in service.

Macbrayne's Poster, 1936

In 2005 in her sixtieth season *Waverley* travels further than ever and each year, after completing her Clyde season at the end of August, goes off to the south of England and cruises from the Bristol Channel to East Anglia, earning her keep until mid Autumn. Some of her predecessors may have shown that paddle steamers can indeed travel far but the *Waverley's* journeys have exceeded them all since she has both visited the north of France and several times has even sailed right round Britain.

It was largely to ensure that Tighnabruaich would continue to have a pier sound enough for a working paddle steamer that the Pier Association was established. While, the Council maintains the pierhead and the original wooden structure the Pier Association's pressure has ensured that local politicians have not succumbed to the temptation of saving money by neglecting that task. Thus, in a short summer season, twice a week the Kyles again echo to the far-reaching beat of paddles and the *Waverley* continues to call on Tuesdays and Saturdays from late June until the end of August.

This watercolour of PS *Waverley* by Ernest Hood has been recently donated to the Tighnabruaich Pier Association. Since the Association was formed in 1999 certain essential maintenance work has been carried out to ensure that the *Waverley* will be able to continue to call at the pier. Proceeds from the picture's sale will be used for the benefit of the Pier Association

Notes and References

1. There is, deliberately, nothing about fishing largely since this requires a study on its own.

2. See Archibald S Thom *Walking in all the Squares* Argyll Publishing, 1995 for a detailed theory on this matter.

3. Frank Newall and Elizabeth Rennie 'The road to the sea at Ardlamont' *The Scottish Naturalist* Vol 109, pp3-22, 1997

4. Frank Newall, William Lonie and Harry M Sinclair 'Roman coastal defence strategy; the Clyde Estuary in the 2nd Century AD' *The Scottish Naturalist*

5. While well covered in many works, a detailed account of Argyle's Rebellion is in Raymond Campbell Preston *No Tragic Story, The fall of the House of Campbell*, John Donald, 2001

6. W E May 'The Navy and the Rebellion of the Earl of Argyle', *Mariner's Mirror* LVII 1971 pp 17-23. Details of guns and tonnage vary from one source to another. Those given here derive from WE May's article. Elsewhere, the *Anna* (or *Anne*) is described as being of 22 guns and 190 tons; the *Sophia* of 20 guns and 243 tons.

7. George Blake *Clyde Lighthouses* Jackson Son & Company, 1956

8. Colintraive Pier was closed after the end of the 1946 season.

9. Details of typical steamer timings. In 1896 G&SW paddle steamer – Kames 06.25, Auchenlochan 06.28, Tighnabruaich 06.35, Colintraive 06.50, Port Bannatyne 07.08, Rothesay 07.20, Craigmore 07.28, Innellan 07.42, Dunoon 07.50, Princes Pier Greenock 08.15.

Return – Princes Pier 16.43, Dunoon 17.08, Innellan 17.23, Craigmore 17.38, Rothesay 17.42, Port Bannatyne 17.55, Colintraive 18.20, Tighnabruaich 18.35, Auchenlochan 18.40, Kames 18.45.

In 1904 G&SW and CSPB began to pool their resources and the services, for a while with two steamers each way, was reduced.

1923 formation of L&MSR with steamer service ending at Wemyss Bay .

At weekends the boat lay at Ormidale and after Kames Pier closed in 1928 the service began and ended at Auchenlochan. No call at Port Bannatyne after WW1.

10. Leisure and Recreation Consultants/HIDB & Argyll & Bute District Council, 1980 'The Strategy for Watersports Tourism in Argyll & Bute'

11. George Blake & Christopher Small *Cruise in Company, History of the Royal Clyde Yacht Club,* RCYC, Glasgow 1959

12. *The Kyles of Bute, Sailing Club, the First 50 Years 1953-2003* KoBSC 2004

13. Hunters and Munro *The Clyde* A&C Black 1907

Once a common sight in Rhubaan Bay – a steam yacht

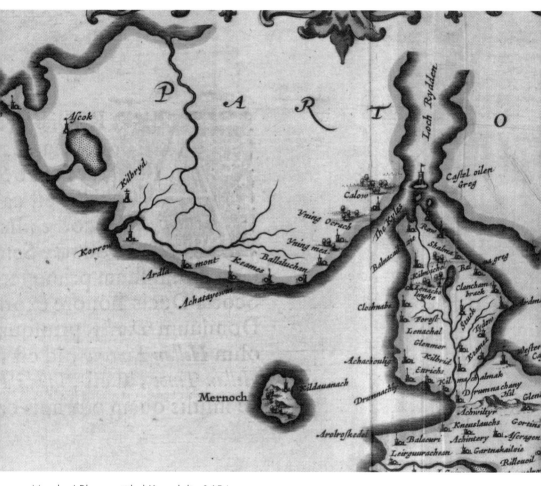

Map by J Blaeu entitled Knapdalia 1654
showing the Kyles of Bute
(National Library of Scotland)

Other Books from Tighnabruaich Pier Association

Tighnabruaich Pier

Ian McCrorie
ISBN 1902831829
£7.50

By the 1990s it had become clear that Tighnabruaich Pier – one of the very few remaining working wooden steamer piers in the Firth of Clyde – was in danger of falling into dereliction. Had its loss occurred the Kyles would have been deprived both of a badly needed calling point for the *Waverley* in her short summer season and also of a local amenity. It would have resulted in the intrusion of something unsightly and even dangerous. Instead, thanks to Argyll and Bute Council which has provided some welcome funding, and with assistance from the West Highland European Link Kist (WHELK) it has been possible to carry out essential maintenance and also to develop the former Piermaster's Office to display items from the pier's past. However, without huge public support given in recent summers to the short cruises provided by the *Waverley* on certain Saturday afternoons there would have been no cash in the bank. Thanks go also to many others for their generosity. Proceeds from sales of this booklet and the book **Tighnabruaich Pier** will all benefit the Pier Association.

The Tighnabruaich Pier Association was formed in November 1999 as a local Voluntary Organisation. In 2004 it was incorporated in Scotland as a Company Limited by Guarantee and is registered at Companies House as SC251095.

www.tighnabruaichpierassociation.co.uk